James Wheale is a writer and poet from Bristol. time for award winning street games company *Slingshot*. He is the Edinburgh Festival Tea Fuelled Slam Champion 2012, Popshot & AITU winner 2012 and Leeds Barefoot in the Park Slam Champion 2010. He is co-founder of Fabler, a digital interactive storytelling platform. Maskboy, the show, produced by the bespoke experience specialists, *Splash and Ripple*, debuts in May 2013 and tours thereafter. An EP of Maskboy, produced and scored by Oscar Lyons is available now from *jameswheale.bandcamp.com*

MASKBOY

This Book is a Time Machine

James Wheale

Burning Eye

This edition published by Burning Eye Books 2013

www.burningeye.co.uk

@burningeye

Burning Eye Books
15 West Hill, Portishead, BS20 6LG

ISBN 978 1 90913 611 3

Printed in Scotland by Bell & Bain, Glasgow

MIX
Paper from responsible sources
FSC® C007785

CONTENTS

INTRODUCTION & ACKNOWLEDGEMENTS

Trying to build a time machine with a witchdoctor was not my intention when I left for Sierra Leone. I wanted to explore how open source educational tools could benefit development, which is how I spent the first few months. I got involved in a local organisation and I met the witchdoctor through his nephew, who also volunteered. On our first meeting, I read his tarot and I Ching and in turn learnt a bit about African magic. After suffering personal tragedy back home and sampling a fine tapas of illnesses, I sought the witchdoctor out for treatment and he gave me local remedies. He fed me thick honey potions. He scarred me with protection magic. He told me that there was a leaf for everything and anything, so I asked him about time travel. He'd never considered it before, hadn't encountered the concept, hadn't even heard of Doctor Who – crazy, I know. We spent a good month designing a costume called a Devil, which is a spirit suit and mask worn by the secret societies that make up Sierra Leone's occult underbelly. Some terrifying, euphoric and utterly bizarre experiences later, I realised that writing this book was in fact the time machine I was after. At first this was a revelation, a way of correcting past mistakes by blurring fact and fiction, of revisiting the most joyous moments of my life and performing god like resurrections on the worst. I could change the past, augment the future, rewrite and rewrite. The feverish talons of malaria, like the inescapable swirls of a bad trip, added lucidity to these audacious thoughts. I ate very little, slept even less and lived in my head, customising memories with parts taken from dreams. It was as unhealthy as it sounds. By the time I left Sierra Leone I was quite broken.

Coming back to England was a mixed process of relief and squaring up to some realities I had evaded. My life unravelled and my bipolarity took control. It took the love of a lot of people to help me through it.

This is where the acknowledgements come in. I went a bit mad for a good year, these people helped me and now I'm happy. It's not often you get a chance to thank people in fancy typeset, so I'm milking it for all it's worth. For being an unswervingly loyal friend, a real life wikipedia (I suspect him to be a cyborg prototype), my magician in residence, a patron of fine cartoons, lord of excellent advice and all round hug in a mug – I thank Al Cummins. For being amazing friends and housemates and for pulling me out of some black, black holes – my love goes to Christian Knight, Lorna Rose, Naomi Harriott-Brown, Duncan Ewin, Kate Cox, Henry Edmonds, Joanna Lane and Josie Cribb. My love also goes to all of Josie's family – I have never met better or more beautiful people. A special thanks to Rebecca Kirk and her family for reading through my work, putting me up when I needed to disappear and for embracing me as a brother. To my oldest friends, Chloe Monday, Charlie Thompson and Andy Wakely, I don't know what I'd do without you. To Rio Thomas and Sam Gage, you both deserve oversized temples in your honour and awards for your dazzling dress sense. To Oscar Lyons, perhaps the funniest and gentlest man I have ever met, thank you for always being there. To the Simons and everyone else at Slingshot, it is a proud thing to work with such inspirational people. To Rosie Fairchild, my producer and dear friend, you have my adoration and respect. To my family, thank you for being everything a family should be: stubborn, constant, incredible.

Consider yourselves all guilt tripped into reading this book.

MASKBOY

CATHY

What do we think
when we stand here
at these platforms
where we wait
still

life on these precipices
still waiting
for the world to move with us
or be moved by us
or maybe
move without us.

Move little currant.

Cathy,
Don't leave us behind.
We can rewind through memories but will unwind with time.
Taped over.

That summer tasted of plums
of glittering nightwater that we'd stood in
we picked berries
in magnolia streams
ankle deep
in amber ripples.

You asked me to feed you blackcurrants.

We drew a map
cut a deal
pinky swears fused
our fingers we will come back, one day.

We made it to the bus and you settled
into sweet summer's sleep nestled
in my neckline
and as we wound our way
through dusk's heavy eyelids
I held you like you were mine
once more.

Only visiting.
I wanted to kiss your mouth for old time's sake
those ripples
last a lifetime.

All tickets please.

Cathy,

I'll build a time machine.

Bighead you called me, Bighead.
Bigger on the inside.
Big enough for the bullshit of my mania.
Big enough for my strange obsession
of crafting cathedral models out of matchsticks
for candle lit storytelling.
For kidding myself

– you called it.

Two crazies shouldn't make babies,
as the saying goes,
in a Bristol accent thickly dipped
and you knew.

You sized me up the moment we'd met.

Yet still
in that sticky toffee pudding of an evening
when summer, the season itself on heat, randy as fuck
tried to breed with the surface of the earth
each person oozing out of the concrete like a sweat bead.

It's as we left it
welled up where we met
same waterhole, gambled wishes and wine bottles.

Here we argue.
Our calling card.
Licked singed fingers and picked old scabs pickled
like petaled love me's and love me nots.
Until bloodied and stuck.

Scratch my back darling, to help us part.
Break a nail

but
your dress
still shimmered
the colours of burning inks
of greens
of blacks
of pale light.
Your eyes
like tail lights.

I kissed you and you cried
you were already another's.

I didn't care and still tried and still tried
like it was fine.

We'll stay in touch through Facebook, you said.
:-(I thought

I walked home my reflection

trying to drown a fistful of words
in his own pool of thoughts.
The last thing you said, the shark in the dreamtank.
The pip in the currant.
The seed of doubt sown. You need time.

Cathy,
I'll build a time machine to give you mine.

While preparing to leave
I collected spent pens like old friends.
I was making up times, writing.

Some things make more sense in isolation.

Cathy,
whether a planet or a single blackcurrant
my world is nipped between your chipped nails

I now ask you
feed me fruit.
Time machines also need food.

This one eats scraps
old lyrics

for lovers lips
I once wrote to hear mirrored
but now mirror as mirrors do,
'Don't you think that it's time this stopped?'
I do.

Cathy,
watch me travel back in time
with a bus ticket and a bundle of blackcurrants
sat in the same seat that cushioned your sleep
a week before I leave.

In the end, it's the white space that defines us.
The time between.
When we sit in these seats,
removed of responsibility for our direction
yet safe in the knowledge we will be there soon.

When we sit in these seats, we think of loved ones
for better or for worse.
We, the passengers, through sun eggs
and as yet undisturbed waters wade.

Some give thanks
others pray,

Next world noh go tan so – *the afterlife will not be like this.*

THE WITCHDOCTOR

I felt like a diplomat
for all those that still believe in ghosts
in christmas
in praying to traffic lights
in those little rituals that we still see merit in drawing upon
for life's little lessons.
He was a stern man
amused by my interest
more so when told of tarot
Jung
voodoo
and tv psychics
the greasy politicians of the couch potato spiritual realm.

I read his I Ching
The Kien
'It will be advantageous to meet the great man'
he tells me I read mine without realising
it doesn't work on him he can block it he says.
I tell him it's just odds.

He tells me of
how his grandfather, gifted him being a witchdoctor
trained him deep in the Forest each leaf can do something
amazing can change everything
heal wounds
transform you into an animal
can take you
from one world to the next
told me how a mirror can catch the reflection of a witch or a victim
to die only by the violence of smashing it into pieces
he can resurrect the dead
he can travel through time

he can talk to gods
but it will cost
for
magic is money and money is power and power is magic and
magic is money and money is money and money is money.

THE DEVIL MACHINE SIDE A

Frankly I saw little difference between the design
and crayon scribbles I used to scratch out on play mats as a child
all two dimensional and transparent,
but I drank jasmine tea as it reminded me of my mum.
A time machine needs the right battery–
look inner child – something to help you sleep.
This machine will transport you from side A to side B.
I said, when asked, that my tattoos were magical symbols,
they had heard I was working with a witchdoctor,
Freetown is place of chinese whispers
and whether by magic or sleight of hand
I slept a little easier.
Still unsure though why, other than
the sum of the odd people I'd met,
I was building a time machine.

Synchronicity? Synergy?

At the start, a souvenir by the end, a lifeline

a guiding hand thrust backward in time.

ANTIGONE

And things fell apart
line by line
as stories often do
in places like this

we were both walled up
in our own ways
by our own hands
palms read
inside out

Oracles
Chiromancers
We longed as fortune tellers often do
not to die by chance

In a photo on your profile
in the only way I'll see you now
on your arm in honest hasty heart felt scrawl
in brash bold lettering:
'Love is all you need'

Antigone
Antigone
At first, I assumed, rainbow rused
slighted by hands surely
a passing comment between pen friends?
'Love is all you need'

it wounded me
made me angry
why did we ever read palms?
When fists are so loud

so ready to say it all
why try?

With open hands hands that say
'Don't Shoot
the world is bad enough without another bullet'

Why try?
When a fist is so universal

In the only way I'll see you now it seemed to me you spoke:
'A fist is a poor man's pass the parcel
never quite unwrapped but always passed
from one hand to the next
The world is bad enough without another fist'

Anti gone
Anti gone
a spell
a spell

I promise
You are loved

And every loved thing is born without chance
prolongs itself out of reason and dies because things do

Only you didn't have to
you chose to
You
The simian crease
My second bluebird

Dear Mr Hughes,

I found your witchdoctor but he wasn't quick enough to catch her.

He wasn't fast enough for her Teddy. Teddy, deep down, we both knew. It was a long shot.

Sincerely,

I asked the cunning man 'surely the second coming is at hand?'
He nodded and replied 'but in her hands, not in mine'

Come back Nimi
The whole world rests
on whether it's a shake of a hand or a fist
but I didn't even get to wave
instead I study the palms of those persons

who are the wrist slappers, button pushers, high fivers, deal
shakers, knuckle crackers of this world
and read in these fist-shaker's palms

the way humanity will end
with the world still

spinning
unflinching
unblinking

another pass the parcel for the universe to unwrap
Whenever

BIG BAD AIR

Charmion
Can you hear me?
The big sleep was coming it was told to us
by our forefathers
and their forefathers before them

No medicine white or black could stop it this time
Bighead knew it was coming
our grandfather had fought it
his whole life

'the Big Bad Air'

it was in his blood thought the Bighead
we knew it was
We-theworld-We
Like a comet
struct the proboscis
breached the Skinthoughtthick
under siege
We-theworld-We
belittled in our condition
by the wagging tongues of other planets
– all previous survivors mind

They prescribed potions
the Bighead took these medicines and we moved it up the Red
then down the Blue

but still there was
a tightness in the Knotinthegutcave

as Skinthoughtthick raised the Hairthatstandsonend
The Ladyhead tried to calm the Bighead

Played him
memories at night
of planets he loved
other worlds
other times –
'be strong
not besieged' she whispered

but still the Heartnotintheheart was straining
was aching
was breaking
Antigone was gone
and the time machine was untested

the Thirdeyeshortsighted didn't relent its advice of pushing
on further
harder
rather than fighting
the Soundsystem
preached 'it'll pass'
reverberating through the Noisebox and the Lungcage
We-theworld-We
didn't believe it
a sour propaganda
the Nastytasteinthemouth

And soon,
the boiler room burst
Self-esteem engine pressure was out of control
the Bighead melted, sweated
the Thirdeyeshortsighted saw
colours behind its closed eyelid

delirious
quickening was the Red
pumping was the Blue

'fever' said the Symptoms
'nausea' said the Knotinthegutcave

'malaria' said the Big Bad Air

'death is coming' whispered the Dark

The Nation of Imaga
was the first to fall
foul of its own incessant panic the I in rot

Civilisation was failing We-theworld-We felt it
but we tried, Charmion, to rally support I promise
but
Skeleton was only worried about going to the party alone
if the big sleep was to take us away
We-theworld-We pleaded for help
but he just sulked
aching

calm
please calm
We-theworld-We cried

but adrenaline surged up the Red surged down the Blue

the Bighead was scared
The Bighead went to brush his teeth as We-theworld-We
marched to war against the Big Bad Air

It was a battle like no other
The Bighead fell to his knees toothbrush dropping
into the bucket We-theworld-We washed in
in that pokey corner of Sierra Leone
Headrushed by a tsunami
of geometric patterns
frothing
suffocating

the Heartthatwasjustamuscle panicked and strained
whilst the Heartnotintheheart broke

again

the Bighead said his goodbyes and lost consciousness
In the humid air
of a washroom coffin
lay the Bighead like a spilt drink

but then
She came to save

came to pick up a memory card

came to bring us forget-me-nots

forgotten-me-knots
to tether the Bighead to bedsheets
in an infirmary

Big Bad Air breathed out

The white grave
The black grave
No man's land

THE DEVIL MACHINE SIDE B

This will be –

a time machine
a can of wupass
a bunch of roses
a superhero
a cure for malaria
a storyteller
a jet pack prozac tin robot
a new prescription from the opticians
a fortune teller
battery farmed phoenix resurrections discounted
all the eggs in the basket
fried
unlaid
poached
and scrambled
a lighthouse
a green house
a lesson learnt
betamaxed
beatmatched
time streams
diet lemon in the refrigerator
a secret sauce
– a time machine
a good lawyer
a magician
a life jacket
a rewind
a rewound tape taken back to the rental store
four elements
one clown

every song I've ever written
maintenance
stamina
playgroup
a dream catcher
a madman
a book of changes
– a time machine
submarine
washing machine
deity
an entheogen
a reason
          to keep on
                    reasoning.

YOU ARE HERE

The witchdoctor spoke lightly
each dreadlocked yellowed
coiling and uncoiling
seven snakes
as he danced over my skin
with a razor blade.

Gave me medicine to take.

Protection magick.

'The Dark will try to eat you. Are you sure this is what you want?'

Yes.
He wasn't sure what our work would do.
Whether the mask and suit
could travel in time
protect me
or just look stupid.

A whiteman hasn't worn one before.
His last words

'Gods are feral things.'

Remember that.

I put my mask to my face.
Climbed inside my Devil Suit
and remembered.

I remembered the moment I knew I loved you.
A year after we'd first met

I found a tiny token of your esteem signed
in a mutual friend's forged identity
to keep our secret
secret

in my wallet
a year after I'd first met you
scrambling scavenging
for chip change I found you
me
stoned
snug in my brothers coat
in the last shivers of springtime
slurring thoughts warm in music
enveloped in headphones
streetlight tan tinkered
sun-bed an ambling man,

bubblewrapped.

Concentrate on this night.

Antigone

when you flew bye

I was rea-

NIGREDO

Listen Said the Dark

And the noise screamed noise
And the pistons of crickets
Whirred and chirruped
And the bat's hunting horn
Struck fear in powdered wing beats

run little moths run
all I can offer are prayers as landing lights...

I ate the moths and the bats and the hunt
and they dance in my belly
they are trapped in the black
Said the Dark
Said the Dark
Can you hear the tap vomiting its nauseas trickle?
Does it drown you small boy?
run little moths run
somewhere there'll be a candle

A candle? Scolded the Dark
A candle? – candles and moths, cannons and spitfires
they are not friends, small boy
Informed the Dark
Informed the Dark
Can you hear the babble of late night radio talk
torn apart by white noise's claws?
run little moths run
somewhere a torch bleaches a portal of sunshine

They run in me
Said the Dark
Said the Dark
And me alone and your candle is dying
drawing its shallow parting breaths.
It laps at my palms and feels my hands at its throat
begging me to choke its glass skeleton for ink
And ink I shall have small boy

My heart rapt on my ribcage
while my eyelids pressed tight
like a lighthouse collapsing into sea teeth and spray
I'm inside Dripped the Dark *I'm the peeling flecks of paint*
In the abandoned palace you call your skull I crawl and I grope
The candle flame looked to me nervously
sweat beads snaked and shed their skins
on the outside of the bottle holding the wick's
suicidal shivers

Deliver me from evil
Giggled the Dark as he waxed lyrical about the candle's last rites
With a final apologetic glance the wick threw itself down the well
it had once plugged

and thus unplugged Pandora's bottle
Which cracked gurgled glowed then flooded
I felt the Dark's wide grin rest atop my trembling shoulders
As he cuddled up, snuggling
To my heart's frantic knocking clawing
like a cat scratching at its cat flap
I lit a cigarette before he could gobble me up

Twos Slurped the Dark

Of course, I replied sweat tumbling out of my pores, terrified
but what if I slept out with the stars and the moon
with his month long wink?
And I thought and I thought where the sun once sat
I felt the warmth from his nap
still nestled in the stone
It must be there somewhere...

'We're tucked up in cloud covers'
came a choir of comfortable sleepwalkers
'sometimes we drift out of storms snug slumber to pinprick paths
for loose threaded sailors, wayward, wayward but that's all'
whispered the constellations
and with that; a million voices faded

Moon! I called out, sweet moon wake up!
A silver slit like a scalpel flick on lead's weathered face
unscrewed itself from the sky
Enough time to blink a weary blink and say
'not tonight my child, I'm tired'
But I'm Dying! I cried
and everything laughed and howled and crooned

Said the Moon
Said the Moon
'you are a child made of water, when that body dissolves you'll
resurface in another so good night small child'
And with that, the Moon made himself a cloud

Nobody want to play with you small boy?
Smothered the Dark
Smothered the Dark

I paper chained cigarettes of slowly dying men
I focused on each glowing tip as they smeared
snail trails in front of my eyes
I felt my lungs convulse and shake
So weak small boy?
Inflicted the Dark
Inflicted the Dark
Malaria does that
Those little parasites are feeding on your blood
Can you feel them digesting you?

My head swelled I felt I was being
pushed out of my body by squatters
Out of myself to be left helpless in Freetown I, the stray

I reached across the table and picked up
a mottled plastic bag
and took out
a mostly empty water bottle the bottom of which
was thick
with a shaded paste of bark and wild honey

Well well well
Said the Dark
Said the Dark
Look who went to the witchdoctor to play dress up as warrior
I ignored him and dressed myself in my costume
its vibrant colours marched forward against the dark
a proud soldier of pattern with its tactics of fabric
it stood firm in the light of that sludge like night
the witchdoctor was close I could feel him
in the dreams of those already asleep

I ate the medicine
earthy in its complexion
I pulled my mask to my face
and he embraced me with sweet affection

‘Tonight we go into the Forest’ Said my Mask
'Tonight we go into the Forest’ Said my Mouth

Tonight we go into the Forest
Said the Dark
Said the Dark
Said the Dark

MY HEART IS FULL OF BLOOD

They tell us we are nothing
but no things are not things
and we're not hinged but unhinged
not winged but unwinged
mortal men; yes
but still something.

Every man here is his own god
of his own world
his own creator dictating his own joy
or his own despair
How can they tell us we are nothing?
They forget where the universe started
out of a singularity
and out of a single ball point pen
can come a universe
so write their wrongs.

Those un-ministers who bring their dreams to work with them
sleeping hard on the job I'm certain
maybe not corrupt – but not working certainly
sleepwalking their way to the top undoubtedly
whilst brothers are put behind bars by brothers for 'frequency'
unable to afford the freedoms traded
in the handshakes of true criminals.
Yes – this a country of knowing smiles
but know this
knowledge is power
and everyday I see people learning to say,
No More.

I've seen great men stunted by the false prophecies, predictions
and clairvoyance of non-prophet organisations

for whom judgement day is everyday
those messiahs
in air conditioned 4x4s
hollering.
We bring change.
We bring money.
We tick boxes.
We solve problems,
but problem solving brings new unsolved problems
while old problems once solved unsolve themselves
in the solving and change either way
changes again
changes its mind
changes back
and nothing ever changes.

Except we train institutions that poverty means money.
And that an ID card is everything
and without one you are nothing.

But you are not nothing.
You are musicians, actors, boxers and drug dealers
comedians, tailors, fighters and fakers,
lovers, writers, 419ers.
I know you all.
I know you dream of better things.
If they say,
'Tell me how are you going to write that record, if you can't read?'

You say
nobody taught me, but drop me that beat
and I'll show you how loud the illiterate speak

Can change come?
Break the mould
hear the reply in your hand clapped cavern echoes
your cave of letters holds turned tables and scrolls
so you say if they say, 'typset, copperplated?'
you say
No
Vinyl Microphone Demo.

Hands here, read back to front
give then receive.
If nobody teaches us to read then we'll teach each other to speak.
Because we pray when we put our hands to our mouths
that each kick drum is a kick to the surface
each snare is a trap avoided
each minute, is practised perfect
each man is his own god.
In each of you I have seen genius,
I have seen poets who don't know that they are poets
whose natural words sting in their raw beauty
whose words inspire without the intention.
I have seen great kindness in the unconscious actions
of street boys feeding crumbs to caged birds
unknowingly still caged themselves
yet no longer biting the hands that feed so meagrely
just sometimes gutting each other in the Dark for space to breathe.

I've seen skill in all the punchlines
in all the punches and in all the healing
and I know that you're hurt and that your heart is still bleeding
that sometimes your efforts go unnoticed
but I want you to know this:

I too had my angel's wings clipped
she too fell from the sky
my heart too is full of blood
and I too still fight for you.

So for want of a better expression,
this intervention will be
televised
publicised
digitalised
vandalised and scandalised
dubbed
distributed
dropped
cut
copied
sampled
remixed
remastered
relistened
reworked
time and time again
repeating the same message:
In every man
there is a weapon.

In every woman
there is a weapon.

In every child
there is a weapon.

In every being
there is a weapon.

Your brain
is that weapon.

Your thoughts
are that weapon.

Your ideas
are that weapon.

Your imagination
is that weapon.

Your expression
is that weapon.

Your passion
is that weapon.

Your peace
is that weapon.

Your love
is that weapon,

and your words will inspire the actions of kings
or the reaction of the masses.

And you will show them
what nothing
can become.

WHERE THE THUNDER AXE FELL

At an open mic
on a Sunday evening
a lazy beer bottle ending
to a first week back in Bristol's knapsack.

I watch a shaking man hold his dead wife's poem
between finger and thumb
he shakes more as he starts to read his own quiet contemplation
on how to best make sense of his new found silence.

Writing is a great way, I tell him.

NUMB

I sit numb in a car
in a service station
just outside of Leeds
watching history shake itself down
lick the grease
from its paws
from its pores
from its poor.

In the spittle of the service station
in the petrol stains in the concrete
in the starlings
in the skyline
you can see it
the pith of people.

It's a rainbow dog
an oil spill stray
an iridescent mutt
a fucking ugly, honest thing,
all teeth.

This is the grotto of pebble dashed dreams
where Gretta, aged sixteen, straw coloured
teeth braced
kissed with acne
crunched herself into the arms of a co-worker's insistence
her burger king uniform lopping like a dog's tongue
across her bare breaths
breathless
skirt risen up like the winter sun
too bright
too early on

she peeped through eyelash reed beds
squinting to see the moment she had been waiting for
to be grown up.
She grabbed and released
clenched toes
grazed knees
gasped
and unclasped her virginity.

Pulled up her knickers
smoked a fag
flipped burgers
went home
and wondered.

All the while the rainbow dog lumbered.

This is where Bradley aged 3
stirred up a wasps' nest
playing in the sunshine
whilst his dad went for a piss
and his mum lost sight of him. In him
it cemented a fear
a nervousness
a nest
that he would later use to counsel himself when he turned bald
and couldn't please his wife in bed anymore.

And the rainbow dog slept at his feet.

This is where nothing happened to Margret
and she had to wait another day.

This is where suicides and birthdays are/have/will/always be
discussed at the same table.

Where nothing sleeps because nothing was awake to begin with.
This is where a man died
in an ambulance
in a car park
in a country
of a heart attack
but no-one knew his name
they only looked once
and the rainbow dog chewed on his bones

and the starlings flocked
and the starlings flocked
and the rainbow dog chewed on his bones.

This is where I fit in
all of a sudden.
Numb.

Holding a static steering wheel for direction.

Now what?

YOU ARE HERE (continued)

-dy for that big sleep too
but now I see shadows for what they are
something to put your back to.

Another, a brother, this time
felt walled up and the Knotinthegutcave
became the Knotinthethroat
rope broke though
Antigone a spell
yours?

I hope so.

Do you ever feel like a jumble sale?
Out with the old.
Next world noh go tan so.

Snow
a fresh start
it crumples cities
from a blank sheet
into leftovers origami
it makes a swan
out of it all

paper is like that too
it captures the vital spark
catches reflections
like a witch's mirror
but not to be smashed
but framed
not to be erased
but saved

a letter by letter mosaic
to keep a time
real or fictional
alive on a page.

A time machine.
I built a time machine.

This time I save.

You are here.
You are here.
You are here.
You are here.
You are here.

TIME TRAVELLERS ANONYMOUS

This time machine is an addiction
I could move forwards
but there is comfort in covers familiar

here you still live
black fruit stained teeth clattering against mine
blackcurrants bursting in pockets busy with fumbling hands
here every love is called back
to the dandelion clock
and explodes in a reversed yellow radiance
sun eggs
sunny side up

take me back
and watch my unkept garden ungrow its knotted ropes
glow like a solar system
peppered with whiskered flower heads that bloom back into
scintillating star orbs
and everything else becomes less
tatty
overgrown ignored
here hands read back to front

flick each leaf rewinding
from tree to sapling
and as if by magic
I can bring you back
in a handful of lines
exploding
in a yellow radiance
laced across your tangerine lit wrists
singing one of the crap songs we once wrote

Antigone
back to her rightful place as a myth.
This is what a time machine does
it makes you an addict of your past

in the moments I saved
I see myself still staring
into the spaces between
still searching

and all that emerges
as time goes by
is a reflection
of an old man
still travelling

in a book of changes
still
unable to change fate
the first time round

only able to change the way
history is written down

Editing and editing
ignoring the new buds
that are blossoming

He looks at me
and tells me to scatter some dandelion seeds
with what breath
I have left

go on,
write a new story

CLOSER AND LESS IRRITABLE

Like stubble on shaven genitalia
take the rough with the smooth
in those simple moments
of pleasure

babes
I'm a suicide case suited to you
and unpacked
I found the light lit
with a match struct off the inside of your thighs
and the outside of my face – graze graced
we have that spark
that sandpaper charm

and it's a true flame
not a lighter, perfect photo finish or electric heater

just real unphotoshopped people
ugly in places
but smoothed out
rubbed down
and repainted
in our own time

let's go on holiday
somewhere shit

so we can reminisce about the good times
rather than try to recreate them

without realising we
distil nostalgia to be bottled up and aged
lying in beds made only to be unmade by making

not a vivid memory
just a contribution to the bank
to something worth saving up for
that feeling

that we're happy

Unbuckle your bra strap
and I won't wear socks to bed
and we'll feel sexy for the effort
even though, we're probably not

And I'll kiss you
then snore
like a trumpet
playing an ode to us
us happy unperfect perfectly happy us

PUZZLED PIECES

Lastly
after everything is neatly away
we slot together in a packed up room of cardboard boxes
two jigsore pieces
arm in arm
cradling the whole picture

until split in transit
one of us to be lost down the sofa
the other
to become a lucky totem for a unborn child's tiny fingers
a mother
to a new future

in another country
reincarnated

whilst I
a puzzled piece of your life
remain
The missing face

in the bigger picture's frame

MASKBOY

Your eyes are two planets synchronised
snowcapped
centred
with emerald jade forests
that swirl under the circuits
of eyelash satellites

a galaxy
pigmented in pink skin
spinning a web of star signs
honouring the goddess
within.

Each freckle is a supernova
pinpricking its existence.

When each freckle
is traced by fingertips,
they line up in constellations.

You're the heavens
and I am Maskboy.

The boy in the bubble big enough for seven billion
donning a superhero get-up to be strong enough to make
an introduction sweating as the sentiment of saying hello
roasts me alive under my clothes.
Under my breath
I whisper,

'walk with the confidence you are a ninja'
but I'm not
so I mumble hello and you don't notice.

Maybe I didn't save you from a burning inferno

like the beefcake ego I turn into during daydream scenarios
but eventually, I made an impression on you
like the first footsteps on the moon.

Sometimes I don't feel I warrant the man
let alone the prefix of super
and I struggle with the application of doing what gains respect
The saying goes life is short
but the truth is
life can be equally as long.
I find myself frightened for the most part,

but if I'm to cower,

I'll be scared with the power of a thousand comic book characters.
I'll quiver in my boots but stand my ground regardless
because you took the time to take it.

I'm amazed that despite the challenges we face
I hold your constellations, tales and fables
between limbs
that buckle under press ups
yet stand up and stretch for the occasion.

Just to contain, what you evoke.

You're like a snow globe.
That when shaken,

sprinkles hope.

You are christmas morning to me and every christmas I wrote:

Dear Santa,
make me a superhero, please,
so I can punch people through buildings and shit.

Give me a cape and let me fly. I don't want any toys.
I'm done playing.
Yours sincerely,
Maskboy
P.S. please don't make my one weakness too weak.

As the weeks and years
rolled on by it was revealed to me
that the decline of a relationship is like kryptonite to me
and whether superhero or superzero
goddess or just a girl,
I felt shot down whenever I heard the words

'it's over'

but I wont let that happen this time.

They call me Maskboy
but only because I asked them to.

Not disguising my identity, but broadcasting my insecurities
the man behind this mask,
is just a man.

but truthfully,
all of us are superheroes deep down

so don't feel ashamed if you feel afraid
fear is half the battle
and to accept that and do something stupid anyway
like tell someone

I love you

makes you a hero

to me.

Admittedly,

my pen still fucks the page whenever I think of you
gives birth to the totems in my scrapbooks
a bedroom full of artefacts,
that inspire under archeological rumblings

proof that once a lunar goddess walked here
leaving footsteps etched in my memory.

Like this,

this is a photo of a love bite you gave me on holiday.
The waiters repeated the same joking phrase over and over:

'the mosquitos are big here, no?'

This is an energy.
That radiates still from the first time I led you up
to my childhood bedroom
and you turned me into an unravelling tesla coil
unearthing sparks between lips and clit connected.

Somewhere along the way
I became a superhero
with the power of lightning

and the rainforests in your eyes, thundered.

And love, conquered.

Even now the hairs on my arm stand to attention
and a heart thought dead is shocked back to life, fluttering.

My feelings for you
still electric in the currant.

When I grow up I want to grow old with you
because we took the time to take it
and hero or no hero,
I want us to make it.
Is it a bird?
Is it a plane?
Or is it an insane search for glory?

No, it's just Maskboy
to the rescue.

I am Maskboy.

I am Maskboy.

I am Maskboy.

I am Maskboy.

MASKBOY WILL RETURN